EMBROIDERY FOR THE CHURCH

A Handbook for Designers and Stitchers

BETTY BUNKER

Augsburg Fortress, Minneapolis

Contents

Introduction 3

1. The Liturgical Year 4

2. Getting Started 5

3. Marking the Fabric 6

4. Mounting the Fabric 8

5. Surface Embroidery 10

6. Couching 14

7. Appliqué and Attachments 18

8. Canvaswork 20

9. Evenweave 27

10. Assembling and Hanging Banners 30

11. Storing and Maintaining Banners 32

Acknowledgments

Text: Betty Bunker
Cover and book design: Hetland Ltd.
Inside illustration: RKB Studios Inc.
Editors: Kristine Oberg, Louise Lystig, Betty Christiansen

ISBN 0-8066-2646-1

1 2 3 4 5 6 7 8 9 0 1 2 3 4 5 6 7 8 9

Introduction

*We will shout for joy when you are victorious
and will lift up our banners in the name of our God.*
Psalm 20:5 NIV

Embroidery for the church, ecclesiastical embroidery, has enriched worship for centuries. Banners in particular have displayed the beauty of this rich art form.

Banners have been used by people of every nation. Armies, royal courts of kings and emperors, and churches have displayed banners. They are mentioned many times throughout the Old Testament; each of the 12 tribes of Israel had a banner around which the members of that tribe rallied, whether in battle or during the 40 years of wandering through the desert (Numbers 2:2).

Today congregations use banners in much the same manner as groups have in the past. Processional banners identify the people who are processing and proclaim the special message of the occasion. When hung in a congregation's worship space, banners help interpret the occasion or season of the church year and add color and interest to the surroundings. A permanent banner displayed in a prominent place might be based on the name of the congregation (Good Shepherd, Christ the King, St. John's) or display the congregational or denominational logo.

Banners are made to celebrate special occasions, such as Baptism, confirmation, dedication, ordination, or Thanksgiving Day. The possibilities for banner themes are unlimited. What makes banners effective is the thought, creativity, design, and skilled work that go into them.

Religious embroidery has a long and varied history. In the Judeo-Christian tradition it begins with God's instructions to Moses for setting up the tabernacle. Many hundreds of years later, during the Middle Ages, church needlework reached a pinnacle in England. Rich fabrics, exquisite thread, and intricate designs were used to create lavish works of art. The rise of pietism, particularly the Puritan movement, dealt ecclesiastical embroidery a severe blow. Many of the beautiful old stitcheries were destroyed. In some cases, pietists thought the ornate banners were an abomination to God. Others saw the embroidery as a source of quick wealth and reclaimed the gold and jewels with which these embroideries were decorated. Yet even during that time of rigid austerity, people continued to stitch for the glory of God. The stitching continues today.

Most of the world's large cathedrals and many small congregations have embroidery guilds. Some congregations commission artists to create special pieces. Nuns of the Roman Catholic, Eastern Orthodox, and Anglican churches continue to create extraordinary embroideries in both traditional and contemporary styles.

A great revival in church stitchery began about the middle of the 19th century and seems to be growing still. More and more Christian embroiderers are taking an interest in the art of ecclesiastical embroidery, enlarging its horizons and using their needles to express their faith. Their embroideries contribute a visual element to worship, helping to create a reverent atmosphere by reminding us of God's love and grace.

1

The Liturgical Year

Choices for banner themes and for the colors selected often are keyed to festivals and seasons of the church year and the colors associated with them.

Many of the customs and traditions followed by the Christian church are inherited from Jewish practice. The ancient Hebrews used a lunar calendar, observing festivals such as Passover according to the phases of the moon. The actual dates of celebrations changed from year to year. The early Christian church also developed under the influence of the Roman solar calendar, with feasts and festivals celebrated on fixed dates. The liturgical calendar that many Christians follow today reflects the influence of both the fixed and lunar calendars.

The fixed portion of the calendar includes Christmas Day; the Epiphany of Our Lord; Mary, Mother of Our Lord; the Conversion of St. Paul; and the days dedicated to the various saints and martyrs. The dates for Ash Wednesday, Easter, Pentecost, and the Ascension of Our Lord are variable, determined by the lunar calendar.

The church gradually adopted colors to represent seasons and holidays of the liturgical year. God had commanded the Israelites to use red, purple, and blue, combined with gold threads, when they embroidered fine linen to decorate the tabernacle. These colors, along with green, became the basis for the colors used by many Christians.

The various denominations do not always use colors in exactly the same ways. But there is general agreement on the meaning of the ecclesiastical or liturgical colors and the days or seasons for which they are displayed.

Blue is the color of love, hope, and truth. It is often used during Advent, the season that begins the liturgical year and starts on the fourth Sunday before Christmas. Many congregations use purple or violet for all four Sundays, although some prefer rose-pink on the third Sunday, called *Gaudete Sunday.*

White is traditionally associated with purity, rejoicing, innocence of the soul, and the light of truth. It is the color for church feasts and festivals associated with Christ, such as Christmas, Epiphany, the Circumcision or Presentation of Our Lord, the Baptism of Our Lord, the Transfiguration of Our Lord, Trinity Sunday, and All Saints' Day. The season of Easter calls for white, though some congregations use gold for Easter Day and for Christmas Day. White is also used for days when we remember witnesses to the Christian faith (saints). Some denominations use white for weddings, Baptisms, and confirmations, while others retain the color of the season.

Gold is used as a glorified white.

Violet or **purple** recall royalty, penitence, love, truth, passion, mourning, humility, fasting, sympathy, and suffering. The color used for Lent varies from denomination to denomination, but the most common color is violet. Other colors (scarlet, red, or red with black) might be used during Holy Week, beginning with Palm Sunday.

Black is the color of sorrow, mourning, and death. Good Friday calls for black or for leaving the altar bare, except in Anglican churches where red with black is used. Black is sometimes used for funerals, although many Christians use white to express the hope of the resurrection.

Red, representing fire, love, zeal, blood, and sovereign power, is the color most frequently used for days dedicated to martyred saints. Red is also used for the Day of Pentecost, Holy Cross Day, and, if observed, Reformation Day/Sunday.

Green signifies charity, renewal, growth, spring, nature, rejuvenation, and life. The color that appears most frequently throughout the liturgical year, green is used for the Sundays following Epiphany and then again for the Sundays after Pentecost or after Trinity.

Other colors sometimes used are **brown** (renunciation), **gray** (humility, mourning), and **yellow** (treason, jealousy, degradation, and deceit, although yellow also can be a variation of green).

Getting Started

Wben preparing to make a banner, you are probably eager to begin planning the theme and design. Other things need to be considered carefully, however, before the banner is begun.

What style of banner would be most suitable for the space where it will be used? Do the surroundings require something elegant or rustic? Is the size of the banner appropriate for the space it will occupy? Is this a processional banner, or will it be hung on a wall or a fixed stand? Will it be viewed from a short distance, or will the design need to be exceptionally large in order to be seen from the back rows? Will the banner be embroidered, appliquéd, or both? Is lettering necessary to carry the message of the banner? If so, what size and style of lettering is needed so it can be read easily? Who will do the final construction of the banner—the designer, a professional studio, or a member of the congregation?

What sort of budget is available? Has the money already been set aside or will it need to be raised? If the money comes from memorial funds, will the donors make suggestions or state preferences? Is there a deadline such as an anniversary or a special festival by which the banner must be finished?

When all the questions have been answered, the designer can put together a project proposal. A carefully considered proposal will include colored sketches, fabric samples, suggestions for embroidery stitches and techniques, explanations of symbols or biblical references, an estimate of the cost for materials and labor, and, if desired, a schedule or time frame outlining when the project will be completed.

Once the design and the estimate have been approved, full-scale drawings or patterns can be made. If appliqué is to be used on the banner, separate patterns must be made for each appliquéd section.

Equipment

Gather together needed equipment at the outset of the project. Fabrics and materials should be purchased or ordered if not readily available at fabric stores, office and art supply stores, or craft shops. Necessary tools include:

- large easel pad of white paper (or brown wrapping paper, craft paper, or butcher paper)
- drafting table or other large worktable
- T square (the longest one available)
- metal meterstick (metric yardstick)
- map pins or thumbtacks
- correction fluid
- art gum erasers
- drawing pencils (both soft-lead and hard-lead)
- black felt-tipped pens with heavy, round nibs
- heavyweight tissue paper
- pounce and pouncer powder
- top-grade tailor's chalk (and/or supply of either yellow or white dressmaker's carbon)
- large sheets of reproducible #10 graph paper (for counted cross stitch or waste canvas embroidery)

Ecclesiastical embroidery can make use of a wide range of fabrics, fibers, decorative objects, and techniques. Surface embroidery, canvaswork, evenweave stitchery, and appliqué can be combined to create rich textures and effects. Specific recommendations about selecting materials and explanations of some of the most common stitches are included with the descriptions of each kind of stitchery.

Colors used for banners, particularly that of the ground (background) fabric, should be chosen with care. Before purchasing materials, compare samples with the paraments and vestments with which the banner is to be displayed. If the banner is to be carried in procession or placed in the chancel, the color of the ground fabric or of the embroidery should be in the same color family as the paraments.

Marking the Fabric

Because ecclesiastical embroidery is intended to have a long life, the medium used for tracing should be carefully chosen. Waterproof marking pens, acrylic pens, and oil paints are often used, although the effect of these media on cloth fibers has not been conclusively determined. A hard-lead #4 or #5 pencil or India ink used with a fine sable brush are safer alternatives. Tailor's chalk, dressmaker's pencil, dressmaker's carbon, and pounce are also acceptable.

Several methods for tracing the design onto the fabric work well. The method chosen is a matter of personal preference. Whichever method is used, be sure to begin by aligning the design properly on the fabric so that the warp and weft on the ground fabric and any applied fabrics remain perpendicular.

Mark the design with both vertical and horizontal center lines. Use a measuring stick and a fine-line pen in an ink color that will contrast sharply with the pencil used for tracing.

Then mark the vertical and horizontal centers of the ground fabric with a pencil mark in the seam allowances for small pieces or a long basting stitch for larger ones. Matching the center lines, place the drawing on top of the fabric. Weight it down or pin it in place to prevent slipping. If the work surface is topped by a cloth-covered soft-fiber board (such as Cellotex), steel map pins placed at frequent intervals can be used.

Prick and Pounce

The prick and pounce method, one of the oldest, is still used by artisans around the world. Although accurate and fairly simple, it is more time-consuming than some other methods.

Carefully draw the design onto a large sheet of paper. Then trace it onto heavy tissue paper, waxed paper, or oiled tracing paper. Make short strokes with the pen or pencil, as if sketching, rather than a continuous sweep.

Next, prick tiny, closely spaced holes along the outline of the traced design, using a size 9 or 10 embroidery needle. (A needle vise will protect fingers and enable you to get a firm grip on the needle. Several types of commercial needle vises are available, or a homemade vise can be constructed by inserting the needle into a padding of folded paper or by wrapping a protective ball of masking tape around the eye of the needle.) The holes may also be made by setting a short-length stitch on the sewing machine and sewing, without thread, over the lines of the design. Although this may be slightly difficult for a very large embroidery, it works quite well for small pieces.

Avoid outlining tiny areas or especially narrow parts of the design with the needle. Draw these freehand either at the final step of the transfer or at the embroidering stage.

Check that all the major outlines have been pricked by holding the tissue paper up to the light. Then lay the fabric out on a big table, making sure the threads are straight and square. Cut out the shapes, being sure to allow for any hems and turn-unders. Whenever possible, use the drawn thread method of cutting, pulling a thread in the cloth all the way through the fabric to leave a distinct line that can be used as the cutting line.

Transfer the design markings with a pouncer (a). Commercial pouncers are fairly easy to find, or a homemade pouncer can be made easily by rolling a strip of felt about 3 or 4 inches wide lengthwise into a tight, fat roll (b). Whipstitch the loose end of the felt to the rest of the roll.

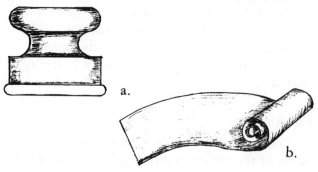

a.

b.

Use the pouncer to rub pounce, a light powder, along the lines of the pricked perforations (c). Make small circular movements to ensure that the powder fills the holes. White pounce is used for dark fabrics, and black is used with light colors.

After gently blotting or blowing away any loose powder, carefully remove the pattern. Using a #4 or #5 hard-lead pencil or a #1 or #2 fine sable paintbrush with white, gray, black, or blue fabric paint, connect all the tiny dots into a thin but definite line. If paint is used, let it dry thoroughly and then handle carefully so the paint will not flake away.

Tracing

Tailor's chalk or dressmaker's pencil can be used for either tracing the design or for drawing it freehand. Hard-lead pencils or paint will make the marking more permanent. Do not use "disappearing" fabric markers; the chemicals used in these pens have a tendency to eat away the fabric.

A light box may be used to transfer the design to the fabric. Tape the design on top of the box, making sure it is squarely placed, then arrange the fabric over it. Match the centers of the design and the cloth, anchor the cloth, then trace the design.

A light box can be easily constructed using a homemade wooden frame. Inside the frame, mount at least four fluorescent lights. Top the light box with frosted glass or Plexiglass set over a sheet of diffusion plastic. A less elaborate light box can be improvised using a draw-leaf (extendable) table, a sheet of glass or Plexiglass, and one or more table lamps. Open the table as wide as it will go, remove the leaves, place the glass over the opening, and situate the lamps underneath.

Dressmaker's Carbon

Dressmaker's carbon can also be used to mark the material. Sandwich the carbon paper between the fabric and the design. Secure them together, again making sure to align the centers of the design and fabric. Using a stylus such as a heavy pencil, inkless ballpoint pen, or a blunted orange stick, trace the design using a firm, steady pressure.

Mounting the Fabric

Even the world's best stitcher will have difficulty producing a fine piece of work if the fabric has not been properly mounted and stretched on a frame. A certain amount of practice will be necessary to become proficient.

When mounting fabric, it is imperative to keep cloth smoothly stretched; nothing spoils the effect of a beautiful design more than wrinkles and puckers. Mounting and stretching is especially essential for silk and metal embroideries, which cannot be blocked because any dampness will waterspot the silk and discolor the metals. Do not stretch cloth drumhead tight, however, because when it is taken from the frame the cloth will spring back into its original shape, creating wrinkles around the embroidery.

Finding an adequate frame is not difficult. Artist's stretcher strips, an old picture frame, a scroll (or slate) frame, or a large hoop will serve as an adequate mount. For extremely large pieces of embroidery, a quilting frame is recommended.

The fabric used for the ground of the banner should be backed by another cloth. This backing cloth is usually a fine grade of preshrunk cotton muslin or linen. Be sure to shrink the backing cloth, then press it to remove any wrinkles before measuring the desired size. (Shrinking and ironing the muslin or linen is extremely difficult; it can be accomplished most easily by sending the material to a professional cleaner, who is better equipped to cope with several yards of wet fabric.)

The edges of the backing cloth must be straight with the grain of the ground fabric. Pull a thread of the backing and then cut along the resulting line to make a straight edge. The backing cloth should be 8 inches longer and wider than the ground fabric in order to allow for a 4-inch margin on each side of the fabric. This margin will be necessary when mounting it to the frame.

Mark horizontal and vertical center lines in the margins on each side of the cloth.

Stretcher Strips (or Picture Frame)

Mark the center of each side of the frame and match these center lines with the center lines of the backing cloth. Stretch the cloth fairly tightly and secure each side, in turn, at the center with a thumbtack or drawing pin. Continue to tack the cloth, rotating the frame and working out toward each corner. Stretch and anchor the cloth in the same direction on each side.

After the backing cloth is in place, center the ground fabric on top of the backing. Smooth out the ground fabric and anchor the edges to the backing with dressmaker's pins pushed straight down through both layers of cloth. Cut 1½-inch-wide strips of acid-free tissue paper, and fold in half lengthwise so that the width of the folded strip is ¾ inch. Pin these strips of tissue over the edges of the ground fabric. With a fine cotton or silk thread, sew a herringbone stitch through all three layers (backing, ground fabric, and tissue). Next, starting at the centers, as before, restretch the working area so that it is taut but not drumhead tight.

Scroll (or Slate) Frame

If using a scroll frame for mounting, machine stitch hems into the vertical sides of the backing, in order to have a strong barrier against which to pull the lacing.

Make a center mark on each of the tapes on the roller bars and on the side bars. (If working with a large piece of embroidery that will have the finished area wrapped around the roller bars, it will not be necessary to mark the side bars.) Match the fabric centers with these marks and pin the backing securely to the tapes. Use a ¼-inch backstitch (see p. 12) with a heavy button thread or carpet thread to sew the backing fabric to the tapes. Keeping the side centers matched, turn the rollers in order to stretch the cloth slightly.

Now measure and cut a length of heavy cotton crochet thread about two and one-half or three times as long as the crossbar, and thread it into a heavy needle. Starting in the center of one of the crossbars, lace the sides of the backing material to the crossbar, taking the needle down through the hem of the fabric, looping the thread around the bar, and bringing it back through the fabric again about an inch farther along the side. After reaching the end of the crossbar, leave the tail of the thread hanging. Start again in the center and lace to the other end. Lace the other crossbar using the same method.

To tighten and stretch the backing fabric from side to side, start in the center and pull the loops of thread tight. Mount the ground fabric in the manner described above, and then retighten and restretch. Wrap the ends of the crochet thread securely around the ends of the crossbars to keep the loops from loosening. Should the tautness of the fabrics slacken during the course of the embroidering, retighten the loops of thread.

Mounting canvas. Canvas is most effectively mounted on a scroll frame, though stretcher strips or a picture frame will also do.

The edges of the canvas should be bound to prevent raveling. They can be sewn over with bias tape, turned under and stitched, or encased in surgical tape, cloth-surfaced tape, or even duct or black electrical tape.

If using a scroll frame, sew the canvas to the tapes with either a short running stitch or backstitch. Roll up the excess canvas at the bottom. (Stitching always begins at the top and works down.) Tighten the wing nuts to make the canvas taut. Although the sides may be laced, lacing may be troublesome with a large canvas because it must be undone whenever the canvas is rolled. It is easier to roll the canvas taut if it loosens.

Mounting large evenweave. Mount on a scroll frame in the same way as canvas, rolling finished areas. Rather than taping the edges, however, turn over each edge and stitch a small hem.

Hoop

Small pieces of embroidery can be done in a hoop. Place material over inside hoop and cover with outside hoop, adjusting the screw so that it fits snugly over the fabric and inner ring. Move slowly around the hoop, pulling the fabric taut while pushing down the outer ring. Loosen the hoop springs after each work session so as not to leave circles on the material.

5

Surface Embroidery

Design areas can be outlined or filled using surface embroidery. The many stitches and stitch combinations, together with the wide variety of fibers with which to work, can yield a countless variety of effects and textures.

Fabrics

Silk traditionally has been favored for ecclesiastical embroideries. It looks rich, wears well, and comes in many different weights, finishes, and colors. Be wary, however, of any silk that seems too stiff for its weight; this can indicate that a chemical sizing has been added to the fabric. Most sizings make the cloth brittle, prone to split or tear.

An appropriate silk can be found for nearly every project: smooth silks with either a shiny or a matte finish, silks with a heavy slub, shot silks (woven with warp and weft threads of differing colors), corded silks, twill weave silks, silks blended with cotton or wool, cloth of gold (expensive and difficult to find) with warp threads of heavy silk and weft threads of flat gold, and patterned brocade or jacquard silks. (Brocades and jacquards should be used sparingly because they tend to be busy and can detract from the main design.)

Linen—colored, bleached, or unbleached— also has long been associated with embroidery for the church. Though linen is long-wearing, it can be difficult to maintain. Even after dry cleaning, linen will need pressing and if it is heavily embroidered, pressing may be almost impossible. Linen must be preshrunk before it is measured and cut.

Cotton may be used. If using heavy, polished cotton, maintenance can again be a problem if the embroidery is very thick. For this reason, cottons with a soft, matte texture, possibly even woven with discreet geometric or diaper patterns, are preferred.

Wool broadcloth is an excellent ground fabric. Drapery materials and many synthetic fabrics are also often suitable for grounds.

Fibers

Silk. Fine work is usually done with silk embroidery thread. It is strong and hard-wearing, though it can abrade easily. Because silk will waterspot, it must be dry-blocked. If the silks are to be used in conjunction with other fibers, such as cotton or wool, it is best to work the areas that use the other fibers first, blocking the piece normally, and then add the silk. (The same approach applies if stitching with mohair wools.)

Stranded floss usually comes in strands of 7-ply that are stripped (separated) and put back together in the number of ply needed to accomplish the stitch planned for that detail of the design. Recommended stranded flosses are Au Ver a Soie D'Alger, Kanagawa Kimono silk, and Cifonda (twisted silks).

Filo, or untwisted, silks are more difficult to handle but have more sheen. They can be more easily controlled by stripping, threading into the needle, and then sliding a very slightly damp piece of sponge down the cut length. Quickly pulling the filo silks across beeswax will also make them more manageable, but the wax will change the color somewhat and dim the lustre. Recommended filo silks are Zwicky, Ping Ling, China, Golden Tortoise Floss, Soie Gobelin, and Pearsall.

Used as is, Kamaito (Japanese flat silk) will lie absolutely flat. Or it can be hand-twisted before stitching. For extremely fine stitching, this silk can be split.

Silks with a tight buttonhole twist are easy to use and give a lovely texture. Recommended are La Paleta, Gutermann, Amann, and Rozashi Plain or Brocade. Maltese Silk, also known as Horsetail, can be used for stitching as well, though it is most often used for couching metals.

Cotton. A less expensive and easier-to-find alternative to silk, *cotton floss* is strong, long-wearing, and easier to work than silk. Generally colorfast, it may be blocked if necessary. Cotton floss must be stripped before threading and stitching, but seldom needs to be dampened or waxed. Readily available brands are Anchor (Susan Bates), D.M.C. Mouline, J.P. Coats, Lily, and American Thread.

Perle cottons are frequently used for surface embroidery; matte tapestry cottons, most often used for canvaswork, can lend an interesting texture to familiar embroidery stitches.

Wool. *Crewel wools,* though traditionally used on linen, may be used on any of the heavy silk, cotton, wool, or synthetic fabrics. Various wools can be mixed with cotton and metallic threads to create stitches with a remarkable sheen.

Metals. Although metal threads are not essential to a beautifully designed and stitched banner, *gold, silver,* and *silver-gilt* thread have a long tradition in the decoration of items for the church.

Few congregations can afford to buy the amount of real gold thread that was used in medieval times. But by substituting the synthetic *Japanese gold* now on the market, "gold" can be used effectively at a cost well within the budget. Real Japanese gold is made by tightly wrapping strips of thinly beaten gold foil around a silk thread. Synthetic Japanese gold is made by much the same manner, using gold- or silver-colored Lurex and either a silk or polyester thread.

Surface Stitches

Surface stitches can give expression to a wide variety of effects and can also be adapted for canvas. Experiment to find the stitches that best render the design. Use "scratch sheets" of the planned ground fabric to test selected stitches with a variety of threads; these scratch sheets give a good indication of what the final stitches will look like.

Split stitch. The split stitch is one of the famous stitches used in English Work (*Opus Anglicanum*). Useful as a filling stitch or an outline stitch, it can also be worked between two areas of satin stitch to form a leaf vein.

To work, bring the needle up through the fabric (1) and take a small stitch (2). For the next stitch, bring the needle up through the center of the preceding stitch (3) and take another small stitch (4). Repeat along the design line.

Creating faces using the split stitch. One of three different methods may be used. In the *medieval* method (a), the split stitch is worked in circles, from the center out, on the cheeks and chin. The rest of the face is filled in around those circles. The brow is worked so that the lines rise over the eyebrows and dip to the bridge of the nose (rather like a child's drawing of a bird in flight). Features are outlined in a darker value. In the *Byzantine* method (b), the brow follows the natural line of the eyebrows, but the stitching line then continues straight down the nose rather than dipping and rising again. The chin may be worked in a circle, but the rest of the face is then worked from the center to the outer edges in upward curving lines. In the *renaissance* method (c), the face is outlined in a darker tone and then filled in with straight lines of split stitch from top to bottom.

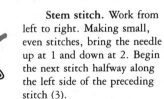

Stem stitch. Work from left to right. Making small, even stitches, bring the needle up at 1 and down at 2. Begin the next stitch halfway along the left side of the preceding stitch (3).

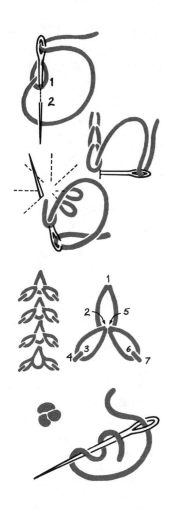

Chain stitch. To work, bring needle up at 1 and make a loop with the thread, holding it down with the thumb. Take the needle down at the same point (1). Taking a small stitch, bring the needle up inside the loop (2). Pull gently on the thread to tighten the loop against the needle and repeat the process to form a chain. End the chain by tacking the last loop down with a tiny straight stitch.

Russian chain stitch can be used for borders as well as part of the design. To work, bring up at 1, loop, and bring down again at the same point, as if making a single chain stitch. Bring needle up at 2, make a chain stitch, and secure with a short stitch (3-4). Bring up at 5 to make another chain stitch, and secure (5-6).

French knot is a tiny knot that can be used singly or in tight groups (for areas such as flower centers). Bring the needle up, wrap the thread twice around it, and then take the needle down through the same hole, holding the thread down tightly with the thumb. Pull gently to snug up the knot and start on the next one.

Woolly knot is marvelous to use either for hair or for wool on sheep or lambs. It is similar to the French knot, but longer. Bring the needle up through the fabric and wrap the thread twice around the needle, then take the needle down through the fabric about ⅛ to ¼ inch away from where it was brought up.

Bullion stitch can be used for flower centers, petals, or curls of hair. It can be combined with other stitches to make a border or design line. To work, bring the needle up at 1. Insert at 2 and exit again at 1, but do not pull yarn through. Wrap the thread around the far part of the needle 5-7 times, then pull the needle through the twists carefully. Hold those twists in place between 1 and 2, then reinsert needle at 2.

Chevron stitch, effective as a main stitch line in designs, can be used for either straight or curved lines. It is particularly good when combined with solid stitches such as the satin stitch. French knots may be placed between the horizontal stitches, using the same or a contrasting color. Work from left to right between double lines. Begin along bottom line, bringing the stitch up at 1. Insert at 2, and bring up at 3. Going to the top line, insert the needle at 4, bring up at 5, insert at 6, and bring up again at 4. Bring needle to bottom line at 7 and stitch to 8. Point 8 is point 1 of the next chevron stitch.

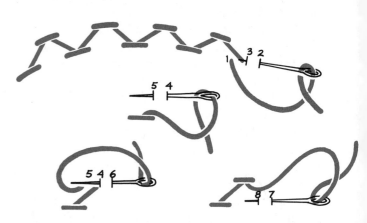

Backstitch is useful for outlining, combines well with other stitches, and can be used to pad the satin stitch. Bring needle up at 1 and stitch to 2. Take a stitch, bringing the needle up at 3, and reinsert at 4 (the same point as 1).

Seed stitch (seeding) can be used for filling. The seed stitch shows up well, even at a distance. Make closely spaced, tiny, uniform stitches in random directions throughout area to be filled.

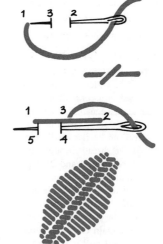

Roumanian stitch is good for making leaves; it forms its own center vein while covering the area well. It can be made to curve, will shade, and can be worked in varying widths. For very narrow leaf ends it is best to start with one or two small satin stitches until the bite is wide enough to accommodate the tie-downs. To work, make a stitch, bringing needle up at 1 and inserting at 2. Bring needle up at 3 along the upper side of the stitch. Tie down with a small, angled stitch at 4. Bring up needle at 5 to begin the next stitch.

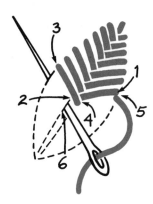

Fishbone stitch is another good stitch for leaves, though the vein or spine is sunken rather than raised (as with the Roumanian stitch). The fishbone stitch may be worked in either a closed or open method, with either one or two center lines, to create different effects. Large leaves should be worked with a heavy thread or cord. Begin with a short stitch, bring up at 1 and down the center to 2. Bring up along the design line at 3 and sink at 4. Work the next stitch on the opposite side of the design, overlapping the previous stitch when sinking the thread at 6.

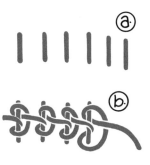

Raised chain braid is a marvelous stitch for a heavy, textured line and can also be used in rows. It shows up well from a distance. The raised chain braid may be shaded from row to row by varying the shade of the yarn. Work the straight foundation stitches first (a). These can be made to follow a curved line and may be worked in a darker color than the chain stitch on top. Then work a woven chain stitch, bringing up needle at the bottom and slightly to the left of the first foundation stitch. Loop the thread from one foundation stitch to another as shown (b), anchoring the stitch to the fabric at the end of the line of braid.

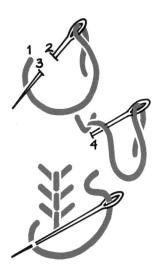

Fly stitch can be worked in either vertical or horizontal lines, depending on the design. The vertical lines can be made to change directions easily. The fly stitch may also be used as a specimen stitch. Bring the needle up at 1, stitch straight across to 2, then angle the needle to 3, carrying the thread under the needle point. (Points 1, 2, and 3 should be equidistant.) Pull the thread through and anchor at 4.

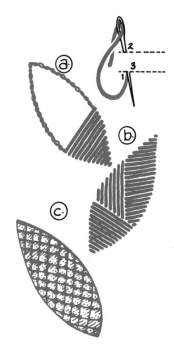

Satin stitch should be padded with a chain stitch, backstitch, or double running stitch for smoother edges and better coverage (a). It can also be padded with successive layers of satin stitch (b). These can, in turn, be tied down with laid threads for a marvelously different look (c). Stitches should be packed closely together, covering the back of the area as well as the front. Bring stitch up at 1, down at 2, and up again at 3, close to 1. Be sure to strip the floss or wool so it will lie flat.

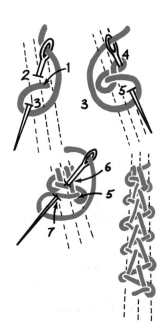

Spanish knotted feather stitch, a good stitch for texture, looks more difficult than it is. The stitch works with many weights of yarn. It shows up well at a distance for larger areas or for creating a heavy line, will curve easily to follow the design line, and can be made to widen and narrow as needed. To work, bring needle up at 1, then insert at 2 and angle up at 3, carrying the thread under the needle point. Pull the thread through. Insert at 4 (between 1 and 2), and again angle to 5, carrying the thread under the needle and pulling it through. Bring up inside the stitch at 6, angle to 7, and again carry the thread under and pull it through.

Long and short stitch is probably the most popular stitch to use for shading. It may be also used for covering areas too large for satin stitch. Work the first row by alternating between long and short stitches. The short stitch should be approximately half the length of the long stitch. Work all other rows in long stitches, each stitch piercing the stitch in the preceding row. In the last row, even the edge by alternating with short stitches if the design requires a smooth line.

6

Couching

Though not difficult to master, couching can be tedious, and it requires knowledge and patience. Knowing what to use and how to use it makes the job much easier.

Passing thread is always laid on top of the fabric and couched with a fine thread (usually silk). Cord or thread such as Japanese gold cannot be sewn through the fabric and must be couched. While a single strand may be couched by itself, it is customary to work with two strands at once.

Couching thread is usually a fine gold- or silver-colored silk. Cut the thread in fairly short lengths (not more than 15 to 18 inches), and wax well before using. (Purified beeswax is available in a handy slotted holder through which the thread may be pulled.) Thread through a sharp needle that has a fine eye, or, if preferred, a quilting needle, though many people find them too short to use comfortably. Anchor the couching thread by taking the needle down through the fabric, leaving a short length of thread, or "tail," on top. Sew two or three tiny backstitches within the area to be covered by the passing thread, and then cut off the tail.

Anchoring the passing thread, called *sinking* or *plunging*, can be done in several ways, depending on the ground fabric used. Thread the end of one of the passing threads through the eye of a #2 chenille needle, then plunge it through the front of the fabric. Remove the needle, leaving a tail about 1 or 2 inches long on the back of the work. If canvas or evenweave linen is used for the ground, the chenille needle may be used as an awl; push the canvas threads out of the way to make a hole through which to pass the thread to the back. Because threads such as Japanese gold unwind as they are passed through the eye of the needle, many stitchers will use a very fine awl rather than a needle.

Do not sink the ends of both passing threads in the same hole. Stagger them slightly, and leave tails of at least an inch on the back of the work. Sew these tails down as the piece is worked, or whip them down when it is complete. You may lay tails along the line to be worked, securing the ends temporarily with a piece of the soft hair-dressing tape, then anchoring the tails with the same stitches used to couch the passing thread to the top of the fabric. Remove the tape before stitching the ends of the tails in order to avoid stitching through the tape.

Couching Techniques

Circles. A circle may be outlined only (a), solidly filled (b), or outlined and then filled with a pattern of some type (c).

When couching a solid circle, stitch down a single passing thread about halfway along the edge of the circle. (Many experts recommend that this strand be sunk after the circle is completed.) Sink a second strand outside the first strand and work it singly until reaching the point where couching was suspended on the first strand. Then continue couching them together, circling into the center of the area. When the remaining space begins to get tight, sink one of the passing threads and finish the area with the remaining strand.

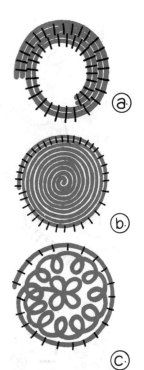

Corners. Couch to the point at which you wish the threads to turn the corner. Leave a loop of passing threads between the last stitch of that row and the first stitch of the next row (a). Gently pull the passing threads close to these stitches, pulling first the inside and then the outside thread (b). Stitch down the outside thread at the bend if necessary to hold it in place (c).

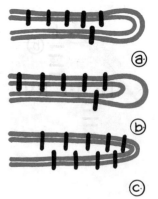

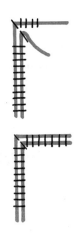

Right-angle corners.
Draw a 90-degree angle onto the ground fabric using a #4 or #5 lead pencil. Couch the passing threads to the corner, securing the outer passing thread with a stitch at the exact corner. Align that passing thread along the angle and take one or two stitches (a). Then, couch the inner thread into the corner and stitch down closely against the outer thread. Use the needle to push the inner thread closely against the outer thread (b). Continue couching both passing threads down the design line.

Reversed (underside) couching. A loosely woven ground fabric is required for this technique. Lay a single strand of passing thread along the top of the fabric. The couching thread, either linen or stout silk, is brought to the front of the fabric, looped over the passing thread, and brought down again through the same hole. With a gentle tug, the passing thread is pulled down into the stitching hole to form a tiny dimple on the back of the ground. This stitch can be worked over padding for interesting plays of light; the brick stitch is generally used.

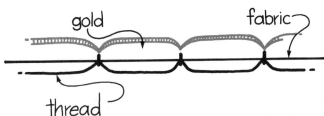

Acute angles. Draw the outline of the acute angle. Couch the passing threads to the point immediately before the corner, leaving a large loop of both strands (approximately 3 inches). Begin couching down the next side of the angle, taking only one or two stitches (a). Cut the loop, sinking one end of the outer passing thread at the exact point of the corner, and the other half of that thread as closely to the point as possible. Sink the ends of the inner passing thread as closely together as possible into the corner formed by the outer passing thread (b). Continue couching along the design line (c).

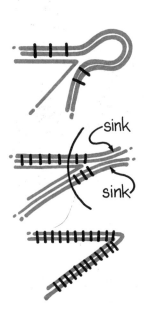

Paddings. Gold passing thread may be worked over various paddings such as padding cords or shapes that have been cut from lightweight acid-free boards, felt, or thin foam padding.

Padding cords are waxed and then laid in the same manner as decorative cords: tack down the edges of the cord with tiny stitches and alternate sides, using either couching thread or a mercerized cotton sewing thread. Dye the padding cords with yellow India ink, so that tiny gaps between the rows of passing threads will not be noticeable.

Small shapes may be held in place with a tiny drop of glue or with tiny stitches around the outside. Couch the passing threads over these, making stitches on each edge of the shape.

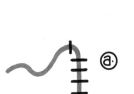

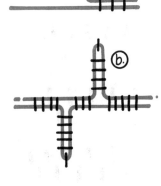

Short legs. Handy for creating vines with branches or branches with thorns, this stitch also makes an interesting filling. The technique requires two strands of passing thread. To form offshoots, or short legs, take one strand of the passing thread and pull it into the direction and shape desired (a). When the appropriate length is reached, couch the strand to the end of the leg, making one stitch at the very end. Fold the passing thread around this stitch and double back, couching again to the main line. Continue couching both strands to the next leg and repeat (b).

Heavy metallic cords. Cords such as Grecian twist, Tosades, and other metallic cords may be couched in three different ways, depending on the type of cord and the desired effect:

(a) on the sides, in the same manner as padding cords;
(b) at an angle across the cord, so that the couching thread falls into the twist;
(c) straight across the cord. (This method is acceptable for woven cord, but discouraged for twisted cord.)

Couching Stitches

Brick is the traditional couching stitch. Secure a line of passing threads with small, evenly spaced, straight stitches (a). Place stitches in the next line between those of the preceding row (b). (For turning corners at the end of a line, see p. 14).

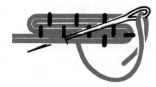

Bokhara, used in the Near East for clothing and wall hangings, creates a woven effect. Work like a brick stitch, but couch with diagonal rather than straight stitches.

Roumanian, an Eastern European stitch that gives a different texture, is worked as a diagonal couching stitch with either even or random spacing.

Cross stitch (see p. 28) gives a nice effect when used as a couching stitch. Cross stitch can be couched over one passing thread (a) or two (b).

Basket pattern is done over any padding that will keep a distinct edge, such as cord, heavy string, reeds, or soda straws. Lay the padding material (cord, for example) so that a space the width of the cord is left between each. (Use a cut piece of cord as a spacer.) Then couch the passing thread over two padding cords at a time in rows of two, four, or six strands. Alternate, or stagger, the stitching when couching the next row.

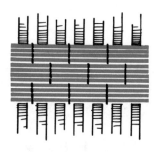

Couching Special Materials

Plate or flat woven braid. Plate, a thin strip of metal usually wound on a spool, is normally laid over a padding of felt, string, cane, or even plastic tubing.

At the place where the plate is to begin, overlap the plate slightly onto the padding at a right angle (1). Stitch down the plate close to the edge of the padding, bringing the needle up at the top edge of the plate and finishing the stitch at the bottom edge. Keeping this stitch pulled taut, fold the plate over the padding, stitching it down on the other side, again top to bottom (2). Fold the plate again, alternating back and forth across the padding and stitching the plate down each time (3-5). To finish, bend the tip of the plate upward, then fold it to cover the padding. Thread the needle through the bent tip and pull the stitch tight. Press down on the plate to lock in the fold. Tie off the couching thread on the back of the ground fabric. Use the same technique for flat woven braid.

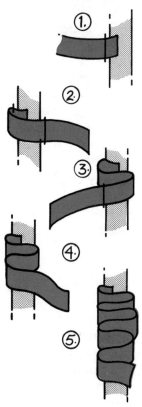

Or nué (shaded gold). In this technique, gold passing threads are laid on the fabric, and the shading, or design, is created with various colors of couching threads. Draw the design onto the ground fabric, coloring it, if desired, with paints or markers. Lay the Japanese gold or cord from side to side, double stranded in parallel lines. The gold may either be cut at the end of each row or else turned at each edge, sinking only at the beginning and ending of each piece of gold or when having to start a new skein. If the gold is cut at either side of the design, sink it after the embroidery is finished; be sure to leave a tail long enough to sink. Couch the gold with the customary gold-colored thread for uncolored areas and thicker, colored threads to match the painted parts of the design. The colored couching stitches may be spaced in order to allow the underlying Japanese gold to show or else packed tightly together to give the effect of solid color.

Purls. Purls are tight, hollow coils of gold, silver, or colored metals that can be couched onto fabric in several ways. Each of the many purls has a different look and purpose in embellishing ecclesiastical embroidery. Purls are cut most easily on a felt surface. (Make a feltboard by lacing a piece of felt around a heavy, rectangular piece of cardboard.)

Pearl purl, the heaviest, must be expanded by pulling it apart before stitching. It may be pulled slightly, leaving just enough room to allow the silk couching thread to slip between the coils; or it can be pulled as flat as possible for a different effect. Pearl purl is used for outlining a couched area or for establishing a design line. It is frequently couched around the outside of attached or appliquéd items, such as gold or silver kid, in order to hide the rough edges.

Purls such as *check purl, rough purl, smooth purl,* and *crimped purl* (a rough purl that is crimped at regular intervals) are made of finer wires than pearl purl, and are thus both more flexible and more fragile. They must be handled carefully so as not to stretch or snag them.

These purls definitely should be cut on feltboard, and, since the cut pieces have a tendency to fly about, it is helpful while cutting to place the feltboard into a large plastic bag or a box that has been turned on its side.

Score the purl at the desired length with the blade of embroidery scissors and snip apart. Depending on what effect is desired, crimped purl may be cut on the crimp for a smooth look or cut between the crimps for a patterned appearance. Carefully pick up the cut pieces of purl with a tweezers and thread them onto the needle as if they were beads. (Using tweezers minimizes the contact between the purl and oil from the hands.)

Check purls are usually cut into small pieces and sewn in a random pattern to look rather like seeding, as shown (a). This technique makes a good flower center or filling for design areas.

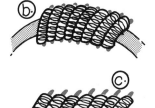

Smooth and **rough purls** are usually sewn over a padding cord (b), a technique typically used for edging. Purls can also be sewn directly to the ground fabric without padding (c). Either of these purls can be looped to form a raised stitch that is held down with another purl (d).

7

Appliqué and Attachments

Appliqué is a technique in which a cutout decoration is sewn onto a larger cloth. Silk and velvet crazy quilts of the late 1800s are examples of this type of handwork.

Materials and Techniques

Cloth is the most commonly used material for appliqué. To appliqué using cloth, cut out the shape, allowing for a small margin on each edge. Turn the edges under at the margin and stitch the piece to the ground fabric. Blind stitching or a fancy embroidery stitch are traditionally used, though machine stitching can also be done.

Leathers are also used frequently in ecclesiastical appliqués. Soft kidskin may be gilded with gold or silver leaf, colored foils, or foils of bronze, copper, or pewter. Dyed or natural suedes, glove leathers, thin calfskins, and ultrasuede are also used. The technique for appliquéing leathers is somewhat different. Cut a pattern from tissue paper, then hold in place (manually or with weights) while cutting the leather. Do not use pins because any holes will mar the leather. Stitch the leather in place with tiny stitches around the outside edges. (Do not turn the leather under at the edges.) Disguise the rough, unsightly edge with a rim of pearl purl that is slightly pulled to open the coils, laid around the appliqué, and couched into place. The ends of the purl will form a smooth butt-joint where they meet.

Lamés (cloths of gold, silver, or other brilliant metallic colors) are wonderful for appliqué, but because of their tendency to ravel they require some pretreatment before cutting. Paint the back of the material solidly with a fray preventative and allow it to dry thoroughly. As with leather, avoid pinning the pattern to the material. Turn under the edges before stitching, as with cloth, but attach to the ground fabric in the same method used with leathers. The edges can be finished with pearl purl, check or rough purls, or with Japanese golds or silvers.

Smaller embroidered pieces, such as lettering (usually worked in couched gold), can be appliquéd to the main design. After the small piece is stitched, cut it out, leaving a ¼-inch fabric margin along each edge. Turn this margin to the back, and appliqué the piece to the larger piece of embroidery with tiny, invisible stitches. If necessary, outline the edges with pearl purl or Japanese gold.

Padding

Padding the appliqué, commonly done with leathers and sometimes with lamés, can create some pleasing effects. Cut the padding in the same shape as the material to be appliquéd, making the padding slightly smaller than the appliqué itself.

For a single layer of padding, fasten the padding loosely to the ground fabric by taking several tacking stitches around the outside of the shape. Place the appliqué over the padding and secure with tiny stitches, adding a rim of pearl purl to hide the edge.

If a built-up padding is to be used, fasten the bottom layer of the padding to the ground as described above. Position the second and third layers and tack them with a loose stitch through the center. Cut the appliqué slightly larger than the desired finished size, in order to accommodate the height of the padding. Attach the appliqué and finish the rough edges in the same manner as single padding.

Crumpled Textures

Crumpled textures can also be achieved with appliqué. Crumpling allows for pleasing interplays of light and shadow, though the fabric may be more difficult to clean and maintain. Cut lamé or other fabric larger than the area that it will fill. (How much larger will depend on how crumpled the texture will be.) Turn under the edges and appliqué the material in the manner described for other fabrics. Then couch rows of Japanese gold, pearl purl, cords of various kinds, or all of the above over the cloth in planned or random designs, leaving puffed and crumpled material between the rows.

Attachments

Adding jewels, spangles, sequins, beads, shishas, and found objects such as tiny seashells is a long-accepted embroidery practice. Such attachments add to the richness of the finished piece.

While few congregations can afford to use precious **jewels,** avoid using cheap glass or plastic imitations; only the best quality materials should be used for work made for the church. Semi-precious and high-quality synthetic stones are reasonably priced and fairly easy to find in jewelry stores, lapidary catalogs, or, sometimes, from the same sources from which ground fabrics are obtained.

Jewels are surprisingly simple to mount. Many of the synthetic stones have at least two holes drilled in them. The jewels are sewn to the embroidery and edged with "settings" of pearl purl. Or the jewels may be attached in the same manner as shishas, if that is more suitable (see "Shishas").

It is often advisable to cover the finished jeweling with a layer of net—fine nylon chiffon or illusion—which not only protects the purl surrounding the stones, but, surprisingly, enhances the luster of the jewels. Dark colors of netting are most effective. Cut a piece large enough to cover each jewel and sew to the ground fabric with minute stitches, catching one thread of the net with each stitch.)

Spangles are flat and **sequins** are faceted. Both have a single hole in the center, and they are mounted in much the same way. If they are to be used singly, anchor each one with a bead, or else hide the thread that secures the spangle or sequin with a cut piece of either rough or check purl (a). If the design requires a solid line of spangles or sequins, apply the spangles or sequins with a large backstitch (b), using silk thread or woven metallic such as a Balger braid in an appropriate color. A strand of Japanese gold or a length of thick, twisted silk may be couched down the center of the line to cover the backstitch (c). Another way to hide the backstitch is to stitch on a short piece of purl with each backstitch (d). These several methods of securing a solid line are equally acceptable but will, of course, differ in appearance.

a.   b.   c.   d.

Beads are best incorporated into high or padded embroidery stitches so that they are not raised above the surrounding surface. Raised beads are too susceptible to being pulled off the embroidery or snagging on anything that might brush against them.

Shishas are small, round mirrors from India. They are often secured to embroidery with colored or metallic threads as shown.

Found objects such as *seashells* and *nuggets* of gold or turquoise may be incorporated into some embroideries. Shells may be drilled and attached as jewels or spangles would be; nuggets can be handled similarly to shishas.

8

Canvaswork

M ost, if not all, of the stitches already mentioned for surface embroidery and couching can be used on canvaswork. Adapting interesting stitches to various types of embroidery is part of the fun of embroidery.

With the basic stitches, combinations, and adaptations, more than 700 stitches are available to the canvasworker. A few basic canvaswork stitches are discussed below.

Methods of using appliqués and attachments on canvas are much the same as those used for surface stitchery, with slight modifications to allow for the fact that one is working on ground fabric with an open grid.

Canvaswork may be the second-oldest known form of embroidery, the first probably being the cross or herringbone stitches used for joining skins to make tents and clothing. Although its exact origins are not known, canvaswork most likely began in the Middle East, and it was well established in the eras before the classical Greek and Roman civilizations. Some Egyptian tomb paintings, in fact, show men and women weaving, on simple looms, a type of evenweave linen fabric especially suited for this type of embroidery. Cleopatra wore dresses of the same type of pulled thread embroidery that is done on canvas today, and many tomb paintings show the pharaohs and their families in elaborately embroidered robes.

This "tabby weave" fabric slowly spread to the Western world. By the Middle Ages it had evolved into fine, pliable, and closely woven material that was used as a ground for the famous *Opus Anglicanum* (English Work). This fabric is perfect for the reverse (or underside) couching and the tiny split stitch that make English Work so prized. A variety of decorative stitches such as tent, cross, Gobelin, herringbone, plaited, and eyelets have been developed for this ground.

While usually thought of only in connection with making kneelers or cushions, canvas is a perfectly acceptable medium for banners, though it can be time-consuming to work and somewhat heavy for a processional banner.

Types of Canvas

Many sizes and types of canvas can be used for stitching banners. Most canvases are made of cotton thread, though the sturdiest and longest-wearing canvases are made from linen.

Mono canvas mesh is formed from single threads. The most desirable cotton mono canvases have a traditional over-and-under weave. The threads used in this type of canvas range from those in which only two strands of cotton are twisted together to those that use six plys to a thread. Because the latter is much stronger, it is preferred for ecclesiastical embroidery. Interlocking canvases are made of a lighter-weight thread that is joined at the weaving intersections so that the warp and weft threads do not move or give. Unfortunately, this interlocking does not create as uniform a grid as the traditional weave, and the canvas does not adjust to varying sizes of stitching yarns.

The smallest canvas that can be used for stitching banners is congress cloth, which is usually 23 threads to the inch and woven of a very lightweight cotton thread with very little sizing. Although it comes in a variety of colors in addition to white, the dyes used are destructive to the canvas itself, making the life expectancy of the worked piece less than embroideries done on heavier-weight canvases.

The heavier cotton canvases come in a variety of sizes ranging from 18 threads per inch up to 7 threads per inch. The more popular sizes for use are the #12 and #14 canvases. Naturally, the denser the canvas mesh, the more detail is possible in the stitching. Therefore, the choice of the canvas depends almost entirely on the intended design of the piece to be worked and the amount of time available for stitching.

Modern linen canvas comes woven with either round threads or flat threads. The round-thread canvas is softer and more pliable because it does not have sizing (starch). It is available in both the 18 and 14 mesh, while the flat-thread linen canvas is usually found in 17 and 13 mesh. Even-weave linens, the type of canvas used in the Middle Ages, range from 40 threads to the inch up to 18 threads to the inch. Usually considered only to be for counted cross stitch, it can be used for beautiful canvas embroidery work and can be appliquéd to canvas with a larger mesh or to areas of surface stitchery.

Duo (double-threaded) canvas was introduced to Victorian stitchers about 1850. It is commonly called Penelope canvas, named for the Greek heroine Penelope, who put off her suitors by saying that she could not consider marriage until she had finished the tapestry on which she was working. In reality, she was waiting for her husband, Ulysses, to return from his voyage; she alone believed that Ulysses was still alive. To ensure that she would never finish, she would stitch all day and then unpick the work at night. Penelope canvas resembles "unpicked" work.

Penelope canvas allows the stitcher the advantage of working details such as faces and hands in petite point, stitched over only one thread, while doing the rest of the design in what is generally called gross point, over two threads. Technically, gross point is a cross stitch.

Penelope canvas usually comes in a brown color called *antigua,* with the most popular thread count being 10/20 (10 gross point stitches or 20 petite point stitches) per inch. It is also available in white, but the white Penelope is usually a much lighter weight than the antigua and is frequently used as waste canvas. Waste canvas is basted onto a ground fabric, and embroidery is then usually stitched from a chart, using cross stitch or a variety of decorative canvas stitches. When the stitching is completed, the canvas is dampened and the threads of the waste canvas are pulled away with tweezers, leaving only the embroidery stitches on the ground fabric.

Using waste canvas allows for an array of fibers and decorative canvas stitches that cannot normally be used in surface embroidery. It is not limited to cross stitch or tent stitch; most, if not all, of the decorative stitches can be used with this technique.

Fibers

Wool. Most stitchers who work on canvas will first think of using *Persian-type wools* such as Paternayan or Woolmasters. Yet while there is a large range of colors available in these wools, they give a rather fuzzy surface texture. Fuzzy-surface yarns have a tendency to swallow most stitches, while the hard-finished yarns give those same stitches a crisp look that stands out from the surrounding background. *Tapestry yarns* such as Elsa Williams, Appleton, Anchor, Nantucket, and Bucilla produce a flat, matte finish on which fancy stitches will show to better advantage.

Several types of wool can be mixed or worked alone. *Crewel wools* such as Medici and Appleton give a lovely effect, and strands of silk or cotton floss can be added as a blending thread.

Cotton. *Perle cottons* produce an interesting sheen and texture. One limitation to perle cotton is its tendency to lose its twist; so, when the thread begins to flatten out into a strand, tie it off and begin a new piece of thread. In addition to their use for canvas stitches, perles can be used for overstitching to give a layered look. Perle cottons come in a variety of sizes: #3, #5, #8, and #12. Anchor/Bates even makes one that is approximately a size #1 that is used primarily for knitting and crocheting. (See the chart on p. 23 for appropriate perle sizes for various types of canvas.) Though the #1 has a limited color range, all other sizes of perle cotton come in a variety of colors.

Cordonnets, tightly twisted French crochet cottons, come only in white or ecru. Yet despite the limited color choice, they have a definite place in canvas embroidery because of their unique texture. They are also useful for for pulled work. Unfortunately, cordonnets can only be used for direct stitching on the smaller-meshed canvases or overlay stitching on larger-meshed canvases because the larger #1 and #5 sizes of cordonnet are no longer available.

Matte cottons give the same flat surface as tapestry wool, but are less expensive. They cover well and come in an acceptable range of colors. Matte cottons mix well with other silk, cotton, and wool threads.

Crochet cottons and *cotton floss* are also appropriate for stitching canvas.

Silk. *Silk floss* works well on smaller-meshed canvases. The flosses have a tendency to twist as they are being worked; they should be stripped and laid over a bodkin, trolley needle, or bent weaver's needle to make sure the threads remain flat and parallel.

Other silks will also enhance canvaswork, but may be more difficult to manage. *Walsh* makes silks sized for different canvases. *Au Ver A Soie* offers *Soie Perlee, Soie Noppe, Soie Gobelin,* and *Soie Platte* (flat silk). *Ping Ling* silks can also be used.

Metals and metallics. A wide range of metals can be used, including *Japanese gold* and the various *purl* (or *bullion*) metals discussed before.

Balger cables, cords, and *blending filaments* are valuable additions to a stitcher's inventory. *Large woven braids* can be used for direct stitching: #32 braid is suitable for canvases ranging from 10- to 14-mesh, #16 for 14- to 18-mesh, and #8 for 18-mesh canvas or 23-mesh congress cloth. Blending filaments can be used with silk or cotton floss or any of the crewel wools. Either the cables or cords can be used as tie-down stitches for laid silk or cotton. These readily available "yarns" are made of aluminized polyester films, have a wide color range (dye-lot differences are seldom a problem), and can be washed or dry-cleaned. They are suitable for cross stitching, surface stitching, and canvaswork as well.

Christopher metallics, which come in both braids and friezes, are sized for 12-mesh, 14-mesh, and 18-mesh canvases. There are even very fine strands that can be blended with other fibers or used for cross stitching. The range of colors for these metallics is small.

Other fibers. *Linen* threads come in various sizes. *Mylin,* a mixture of flax (linen), polyacrylic, and viscose (rayon), gives a tweeded look. *Mardi Gras* substitutes cotton for flax and has a nubby, flat sheen appearance. *Overdyed Appleton, Medici,* and *Paternayan crewel wools* are available for interesting shading effects.

Shading. Crewel wools, silk floss, and cotton floss can be blended together for ombré shading. The silk and cotton are especially good for shading flesh, but can be used for clothing, too. With only three shades of one color of wool, seven shades can be produced, each subtly flowing into the other, when blended as follows (listed dark to light):

- 3 strands dark;
- 2 strands dark and 1 strand medium;
- 2 strands medium and 1 strand dark;
- 3 strands medium;
- 2 strands medium and 1 strand light;
- 2 strands light and 1 strand medium;
- 3 strands light.

With Medici crewel wools, this ombré shading will work only on 18-mesh canvas. Appleton wools can be used on 14-mesh canvas.

Stranded floss is better than wool for showing flesh tones. Stranded floss requires more than three shades to look natural. Do not use the peachy shades for flesh; they always come out looking orange and unnatural. Start with basic ecru (Anchor #387 or D.M.C. Ecru) for highlighted areas. Depending on the desired effect, the other colors can be three or four shades of either "Linen" sequence or "Fawn" (soft rose-brown) sequence. For linen colors add Anchor #390, #391, #392, and #393 to the ecru. The fawn colors begin with Anchor #933 or D.M.C. #543, then progress through Anchor #376, #378, and #936, or D.M.C. #842, #841, and #632. To add a pinkish color to the cheeks and lips, a strand or two of "Salmon" (Anchor #6 or D.M.C. #754) mixed with the second-lightest flesh shade will do the trick without looking too harsh. Shading the lips by mixing in Anchor #8 and/or #9 (D.M.C. #353) will give a more natural look and will help to separate the upper and lower lips. Corresponding colors can be found in the various silks on the market. This method of blending also works well for surface stitchery, usually with split stitch or long and short stitch.

Estimating Needs

Canvas. Figuring how much canvas will be required is fairly easy. Determine the final length and width of the finished item; then allow for a margin of blank canvas at least 1½ to 2 inches wide on each side so the canvas can be blocked easily.

Yarn. Estimating the amount of yarn for a project is more difficult, requiring careful figuring. Because dye lots can vary greatly, it is important to buy enough of each color to cover the required area.

The following table gives yardages per square inch for continental or basketweave stitches. Figuring yardages for decorative stitches is much more difficult. The most accurate method is to actually work samples of the stitches using swatches of the intended canvas and to measure the amount of yarn used for each sample. (Allow for generous waste knots). Then figure the yardage needed for each stitch. Bear in mind, however, that this estimate will still be rough, because seldom do two people use exactly the same amount of yarn. Increasing the estimate by at least 25 percent is recommended to ensure enough matching yarn to complete the project.

Canvas Size	Number of Stitches	Yardage per sq. Inch	Tapestry Wool	Persian Wool	Crewel Wool	Perle Cotton	Floss
#7	49	1 yard	2 strands	6 strands		3 strands #3	
#10	100	1¼ yards	1 strand	3 strands	5 strands	3 strands #5	18 plys
#12	144	1½ yards	1 strand	2 strands	4 strands	1 strand #3	12 plys
#14	196	1¾ yards	1 strand	2 strands	3 strands	2 #5 1 #3	9 plys
#16	256	2 yards	1 strand	1 strand	2 strands	2 #8 1 #5	6 plys
#18	324	2¼ yards	1 strand	1 strand	2 strands	1 strand	6 plys

Canvas Stitches

When stitching canvaswork, always pull the needle straight down and straight up through the canvas. Avoid using the scoop motion often used in sewing: It not only destroys the shape of the canvas, but it is difficult to maintain an even tension on the stitches, resulting in an undesirable high/low effect.

Always use waste knots when working canvas stitches. To stitch using a waste knot, tie a large, loose, two-handed knot at the end of the yarn. Take the needle and thread down through the canvas, leaving the knot on the top surface. (The distance left between this knot and the beginning of the stitching depends on the type of stitch being used. If it is a tent or basketweave stitch, leave only about a ½-inch runner on the back of the canvas. With larger stitches, such as Rhodes

or waffle, a long tail will be needed in order to make sure the thread is securely worked into the backside.)

Place the knot on an oblique angle to the beginning of the stitch, usually to the lower left. As you stitch, work each stitch through the tail (*not* over it). In this way, the tail completely disappears and it is permanently anchored. Oblique placement produces smoother surfaces, front and back, than the generally accepted right-angle placement. Right-angle placement produces tiny, hard knots on the back as well as thickening of areas in which new lengths of yarn are begun close together.

Each length of yarn should also end with a waste knot. Leave enough yarn to bring the thread to the front of the canvas and tie into a knot. As the work progresses and the hole occupied by the knot is needed for a stitch, pull the knot tightly away from the canvas and clip off as closely to the surface as possible, letting the thread disappear into the stitching on the back. Because wool, perle cottons, cordonnets, and most of the metallics have more elasticity than silk or cotton floss, the ends will more easily disappear beneath the back of the stitches. Floss requires a harder pull in order not to leave a slight fuzz on either the front or back of the canvas.

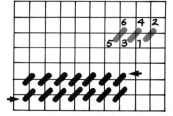

Continental or tent stitch provides a good backing and wears well. It takes its name *tent* from the word *tentre*, French for the frame used for working canvas and other embroideries. This diagonal stitch is formed over one canvas mesh. Start at the upper right, bringing the needle up at 1 and down at 2. Work from right to left; when the row is finished, leave the needle at the back of the fabric, turn the canvas upside down, and work in the same manner as the first row. If you prefer not to turn the canvas, simply work the stitch from top to bottom on alternate rows. This stitch pulls the canvas out of shape, and the canvas will need to be treated with rabbit glue after blocking in order to retain its shape.

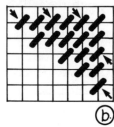

Basketweave or **diagonal tent stitch** takes its name from the woven effect of the back of the stitch. It gives a flat, smooth, tight surface that is a perfect foil for textures produced by either fancy fibers or stitches. Form corner as illustrated (a). Then work stitches in diagonal rows, alternately down, then up the canvas. Avoid working two consecutive rows in the same direction by working all the down rows over the vertical canvas threads (the warp thread over the weft thread), and all the up rows over the horizontal canvas threads (b). Like the continental, this stitch will also pull the canvas slightly out of shape, though not as badly.

Cross stitch see p. 28.

Upright cross stitch. Tough, hard-wearing, and difficult to snag, this stitch is good for either detail or grounding though it can be hard to work with a heavy yarn. The stitch is especially effective when done in two colors. The backing tends to be a little uneven, but is fairly good nonetheless. Work odd rows from left to right, and even from right to left, starting at the upper left.

left to right

right to left

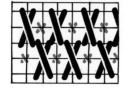

one color

two colors

Double stitch gives a neat, woven effect. It is good for detail or background, has excellent backing, but is slow to work (especially in two shades). Stitch the large crosses over three horizontal threads and one lengthwise thread. Center the small stitches between, working over one thread horizontally and vertically. If worked in shades of one color, the stitch creates a tweedy look. If done in two shades, work all the large crosses first, leaving a lengthwise thread between the stitches; work the small crosses in a second shade.

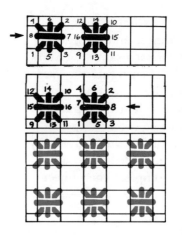

Smyrna cross (leviathan). This bulky, knobby, tough, hard-wearing stitch has good backing and is hard to snag. Excellent for detail, border, or grounding, it looks better in tapestry wool than in Persian. Work a traditional cross stitch first, then work an upright cross stitch on top. Work alternately left to right, then right to left. (Notice that when working the even rows, the last stitch (7/8) of each cross will be worked left to right rather than right to left, as worked in the odd rows.)

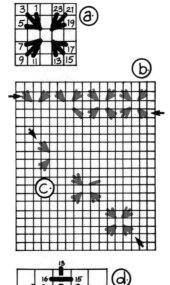

Triple leviathan may be worked either as a specimen stitch (a) or in horizontal or diagonal rows (b, c). It has a good backing, is great for large detail or borders, and is not easy to snag. This is also a useful stitch for a diaper pattern. Using a gold thread for the upright crosses gives a rich effect, and a specimen worked in two colors gives the appearance of a Tudor rose. (The center upright cross can be worked in yellow, or five French knots in yellow can be used instead, to enhance the flower effect.) Work the diagonal clusters of stitches first, then add the crosses (d).

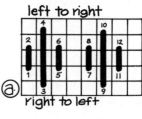

left to right

right to left

Hungarian (Point d' Hongrie). Good for detail, grounding, or borders, this stitch has fair backing, is quick to work up, and does not snag easily. In borders it can be mitered at the corners in much the same manner as four-way Bargello. (See p. 25.) Work the short stitches over two threads and the long stitches over four. Leave one mesh between each Hungarian stitch (a). When working the next row, place the long stitch of each Hungarian in this space (b).

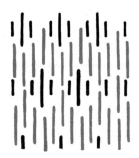

Hungarian ground. With an interesting texture for large detail, border, or grounding, this stitch shows especially well if done in two shades or colors. It is useful for depicting grass in a landscape. Not easily snagged unless worked on very large-mesh canvas, it works up quickly and has a good backing. To work, alternate rows between regular Hungarian and a straight stitch over four threads. Choose a yarn fat enough to cover, and do not pull the stitch too tightly, or the canvas will show through.

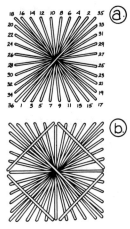

Rhodes. This bulky stitch works well for borders or a large overall abstract design. It shows well from a distance, is effective in metallics, and can be worked in some variations. The backing is good. Work a square area over an even number of mesh. Stitch diagonally across the square, beginning each stitch one thread to the right of the preceding and ending it one thread to the left (a). The stitches will overlap in the center. The stitch can be worked with tie-downs on the corners to lessen its vulnerability to snagging (b).

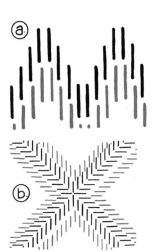

Florentine (Bargello). Another good stitch for large details, borders, and backgrounds. Florentine stitch patterns are created with long, straight stitches that form a zigzag pattern (a). If done as a four-way Bargello, in which the overall design is produced by working triangular quarters of the design at right angles, it can be used to create interesting crosses (b). These crosses can be done on small canvas and appliquéd onto larger-mesh canvas. The stitch can be worked in only one color for a background, but it is more traditional to use at least four shades.

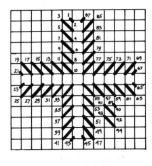

Counted-cross stitch (no-name stitch). Seldom seen, this stitch is wonderful for borders or for an overall pattern in either a solid color (in which it looks like brocade) or in gradations of one color. It can be used as a background. The stitch has several variations, and it can also be combined with other stitches.

Counted cross stitch can be worked as a background (a and b), with flat stitch or flat mosaic (c), or with Cashmere stitch (d). It can also be worked as a border (e). For horizontal borders, work the top halves of the crosses first, and work back to complete the bottom halves. For vertical borders, stitch the outer halves of the crosses first.

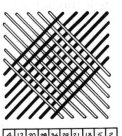

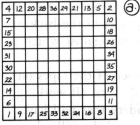

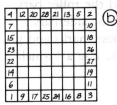

Waffle (Southern cross, Mexican cross, Norwich, or crossed plait). This stitch will snag unless done in a small size on small-mesh canvas. But it gives a wonderful effect and shows well from a distance. It can be used as a specimen, very large detail, or overall pattern. The backing is poor. Work with diagonal stitches as illustrated, being sure to weave stitch 36 (a), 28 (b), or 20 (c) under stitch 29 (a), 21 (b), or 13 (c) in order to achieve a completely woven look.

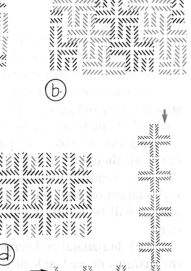

Buttonhole stitch. Perfect for outlining an area, the buttonhole stitch (a) is much easier to work on canvas than on a fabric ground. The stitch is also good for filling detail areas if done as a group of touching circles (b), the centers of which may be filled with French knots or with beads of various sizes. To work, bring needle up at 1, insert at 2, and exit at 3, carrying yarn under the needle and then pulling tight.

The detached buttonhole (c) is probably one of the best ways to attach jewels, mirrors, and found objects (see p. 19) to canvas. To work, lay a line of backstitch at the top of the area to be worked. Bring the needle up to the top of the cloth and slip under the first backstitch, then curl it over the stitch, bring the needle over to the next stitch, and repeat.

Flat stitch (flat Scotch) is good for large detail, borders, or overall designs. It has the advantage of being able to expand and contract. Areas of different sizes can be combined for dazzling effect. If the stitches are too long they are susceptible to snagging, so care must be used when deciding the size. The overstitching helps the snagging problem somewhat. The overstitch, if used, is stitched on the opposite diagonal and covers only half the stitch. It should be worked in a contrasting shade.

Flat mosaic. A lovely stitch, flat mosaic is good for detail, borders, or ground. Though mosaic tends to pull the canvas, by working it as a flat stitch in mirror images, what pulls it out in one direction will pull it back when the stitch is worked in the alternate direction. Flat stitches should always be worked on the diagonal; the backing is better, and it is easier to put in the waste knots. The flat mosaic can be very effective if it is combined with an upright cross in a contrasting color or fiber, especially a metallic thread.

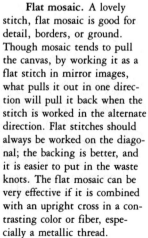

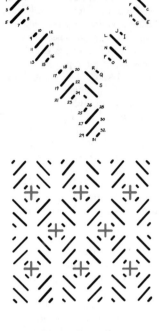

Flat Cashmere covers a larger area and works up a little more quickly than flat mosaic. It is worked in the same diagonal method as the flat stitch. Upright crosses or large French knots can also be added to this stitch; crosses are especially nice in metallic thread. An interesting change of texture is created in adjoining areas of detail if one is done in flat mosaic and one on flat cashmere, either with or without the upright cross.

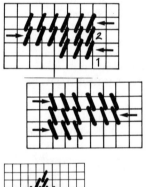

Encroaching Gobelin is a popular stitch that is wonderful for shading. It can be worked to slant to the left or right and can change direction very easily, making it an excellent stitch for clothing, leaves, and other curving shapes. Because it will distort the canvas badly if pulled too tightly, it is a bad background stitch. It must be worked in both directions to counteract the pull. The stitch creates its own shading if worked in one color because of the play of light on the left and right slants. If used for a leaf, work a backstitch down the lap line to reinforce the appearance of a vein.

Diagonal weaving is excellent for details, borders, or backgrounds; it has a great texture and will not snag. It is especially nice when done with metallics. Working a large area with this stitch can be rather slow, however.

The short list above barely skims the surface of the many stitches that can be used. The *long-armed cross, rice stitch, eyelets* of different types, *woven cross, brick stitch, French stitch, Parisian,* and any of the several variations of *chain stitch* are some of the others that can be used. Examine the stitches to see what shapes they suggest.

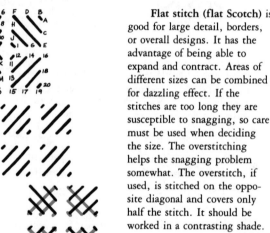

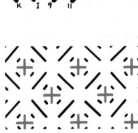

9

Evenweave

Evenweave *historically has been used for both church and secular embroideries. Though many people believe that evenweave embroidery is limited to cross stitch, a wide variety of*

evenweave stitches and techniques exist. Many canvaswork stitches can also be worked on evenweave fabric, and virtually any stitch or technique that is used for surface embroidery can be adapted for use on canvas or evenweave fabrics. In the Middle Ages, the very fine, pliable, and closely woven evenweave linens that were used for grounds were perfect for the reverse couching and the tiny split stitch that made English Work so prized.

Fabric

Over the many centuries evenweave fabric and stitchery have evolved differently in various parts of the world. Fine linens have been used throughout most of the Middle East and Europe, and ancient Nordic embroideries used wools. Cotton evenweave fabrics such as **Aida cloth** and **Hardanger** originated in the Scandinavian countries and have become popular in the United States, England, and Western Europe. (The stitch used on them now is usually limited to a simple cross stitch.) Most evenweaves today are cotton, though some are blended with linen or a synthetic. Evenweaves are available in every color needed to reflect the seasons of the liturgical year.

Techniques

Assisi work. This well-known evenweave technique takes its name from Assisi, Italy, where it is thought to have been developed by the nuns of the Convent of St. Francis. Although none of the earliest pieces of Assisi work still exist, records indicate this type of embroidery has been done since the late 14th century. Several museums have examples of Assisi work on burses and altar frontals dating from the 16th and 17th centuries.

Traditionally Assisi is worked on fine, cream-colored linen with bright red, bright blue, or black silks with stitches such as long-legged cross and Italian cross stitch. Recently it has also been worked in cotton floss on evenweave linen, Aida cloth, or Hardanger fabric. Simple cross stitch is commonly used on American pieces of Assisi.

While Assisi work looks very elaborate and complicated and does take time to execute, the technique is very simple. Outline the design in backstitch or in Holbein stitch (double running), leaving the fabric inside these outlines unworked. Fill in the background with cross stitch or one of its variations to give the look of a photographic negative. As with any type of stitchery used for ecclesiastical embroidery, avoid tiny and intricate motifs. These motifs do not show well at a distance.

Blackwork. Thought to have originated with the Moors, who later brought it to Spain, blackwork is another acceptable technique for ecclesiastical embroideries. Worked with a Holbein stitch, blackwork historically has been done on fine, closely woven linen with a single, fine black silk thread, but modern versions often use cotton floss on an evenweave. It is especially suitable for the Lenten season. Use the traditional black thread on white or cream linen, or try red or violet thread on a natural, pale beige, or ecru fabric.

Evenweave Stitches

Cross stitch, backstitch, and Holbein stitch (double running) are the most commonly known stitches for counted-thread embroideries. Additionally, many of the canvas stitches can work well on evenweave grounds.

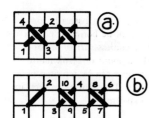

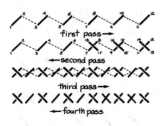

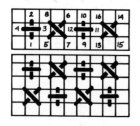

first pass →

← second pass

third pass →

← fourth pass

Cross stitch. One of the oldest known stitches, cross stitch is quick to work. On mono canvas each cross can be done separately before moving to the next one (a), but on evenweave fabrics another approach is better. Stitching left to right, work a row of diagonals across the area. Return with the opposite diagonal to finish the stitches (b). The return brings the needle and thread back to the beginning of the next row. A third method, the alternate cross stitch (c), makes the worked area reversible. It does, however, take longer to work because each row requires four passes.

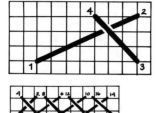

St. George and St. Andrew is a combination of upright cross (see p. 24) and the cross stitch that gives texture to any design area. It can be worked in two shades of one color for added interest. To work, merely alternate between the two stitches.

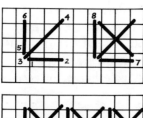

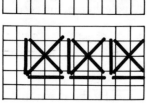

Long-legged cross stitch (long-armed cross, plaited Slav stitch, twist stitch, or Portuguese stitch). One of the traditional Assisi stitches, this stitch works well for filling detail areas. It has nice texture, covers quickly, and is easy to work. It is also effective on canvas. Work so that the first arm of the cross is longer than the second.

Italian cross stitch (two-sided Italian cross, arrowhead cross, or Italian stitch). Frequently found in Assisi work, this dense, textured stitch can be used on either canvas or evenweave fabrics. It quickly covers a large area. To work, make a stitch along the baseline (1/2). Then, bringing the needle up again at 1, take a diagonal stitch (3/4) that ends directly above 2. (Points 1, 2, 4, and 6 should be equidistant.) Bring the needle up again and make a vertical stitch (5/6). Then complete the cross with a diagonal stitch (7/8). Begin the next Italian cross along the baseline directly to the right of the preceding cross stitch.

Woven cross stitch. Of the several versions of this stitch, two are included here. Both cover large areas quickly and add texture to any design. With either of these versions, be sure to weave the last stitch under the existing stitch to achieve a complete woven look. Version a: 7/8 under 1/2; version b: 11/12 under 5/6.

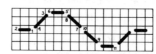

Backstitch. While already described with the surface stitches (see p. 12), the backstitch is even easier to work on canvas or evenweave. It is used for outlining, especially in Assisi and blackwork, and for making fine lines in smaller counted-thread embroideries.

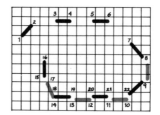

Holbein stitch (double running). Particularly associated with blackwork, Holbein is also used in Assisi and other types of embroidery. It is a simple double running stitch that makes the embroidery reversible, and is excellent for outlining design areas. It derives its name from the portrait painted by Hans Holbein the Younger. Many of his portrait subjects, including King Henry VIII, wore clothing decorated with blackwork, which he faithfully reproduced stitch by stitch. To work, make one pass with evenly spaced running stitches. Then turn the work and make another pass along the same line, stitching over the spaces left by the first pass. Enter and exit at the same holes.

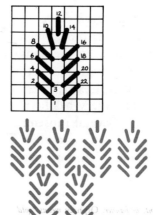

Leaf stitch. Nice when worked as a solid area, this stitch can also be used as leaves for a tree or combined with triple leviathan to make a flower with leaves. Work each leaf stitch counterclockwise with small diagonal stitches along both sides. Make a vertical stitch at the apex of each leaf.

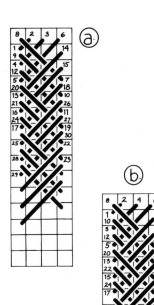

Pointe de Tresse. This makes a handsome braid that could be an orphrey* all by itself. It is useful for dividing bands of designs. It tends to be a little bulky, especially in wool on canvas. Three colors of thread are needed in order for this stitch to show up well. Metallic threads, such as one silver thread and two distinct shades of gold, are recommended. The number of crossings of each color can be increased from three to six, if needed. Method a has a lighter back but is not as smooth on top, while method b makes a heavy back, but covers better.

Darning stitch (Kogin). This simple stitch, basically rows of running stitches of any desired length, could be boring if not for the fun involved in developing an almost endless variety of patterns. The length of the stitches and the amount of blank fabric left between create the patterns. Pattern lines can be repeated or staggered, depending on the desired effect. They can be worked in horizontal, vertical, or diagonal lines. Experiment.

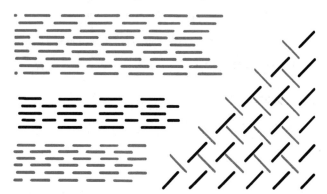

*A band of embroidery on a parament, vestment, or banner. Orphrey means "gold embroidery," and is traditionally worked with gold, silver, and gilt threads.

10

Assembling and Hanging Banners

Though stitchers may feel a sense of completion after all the embroidery work for a banner has been done, the project is not finished until the banner is assembled and hung.

Putting the Banner Together

When all the embroidery and appliqué is finished and the banner is complete, remove the fabric from its frame. Trim the backing cloth so that it is 1¼ inches smaller vertically and horizontally than the overall size of the ground fabric. This will create a ⅝-inch seam allowance on each side.

Inner lining. Make inner lining of sailcloth, which will help prevent the banner from sagging and rippling. Preshrink the sailcloth before cutting it. Cut the sailcloth the same size as the backing cloth. Then cut a lining (of lightweight silk, cotton, or synthetic material in a matching or contrasting color) to the exact size of the ground fabric.

Lay the banner face down on the finishing table and place the sailcloth inner lining over the wrong side of the banner. Match the edges of the inner lining to the seam allowance lines of the banner. Trim off the corners of the ground fabric at an angle, being careful to stay within the seam allowance. (Dab these corners with fabric glue if necessary to avoid any raveling.) Then turn the seam allowance back over the inner lining, mitering the corners. Baste into place. (If edges are shaped rather than straight, clip the seam allowances as necessary, then baste.)

Ground fabric. Now turn the banner face up. Anchor the ground fabric to the inner lining by stabbing a needle straight through from the back of the inner lining and taking a tiny stitch at the outline of the main design. Stab through to the back, move the needle 1 or 2 inches, and stab back to the front again. Tack in this manner all the way around the design and tie off firmly on the back of the inner lining. Some tacking will probably be needed within the designs as well.

Fringes. If a fringe is to be used at the bottom of the banner, attach it now, being careful not to stretch it too tightly. Position the heading of the fringe over the bottom edge of the banner front and sew it on firmly, stitching through the ground fabric, the inner lining, and the fringe heading. Turn the cut ends of the fringe to the back and anchor firmly.

Sleeves. If the banner is to be suspended by loops, or "sleeves" as they are more properly known, place the banner face down and mark where the sleeves are to be attached. (If the banner is to be used for processions, the sleeves should be placed on either side of the hook on the staff, leaving a space in the center for this hook.) Determine how many sleeves are needed and how wide and long they must be. Keep in mind the maximum distance the sleeves can be from each other without causing the banner to sag and the diameter of the rod on which they will be suspended. Remember that the sleeves must be doubled to make the loops. The sleeves are usually made of the ground or border fabric. Since they will be self-lined, cut them twice as wide as the desired finished measurement, adding ⅝-inch seam allowances to the ends and sides of each sleeve strip. Then cut a strip of inner lining the same size as the finished sleeve and lay it lengthwise in the center of the fabric strip. Turn under the side seam allowances of the sleeve and baste. Fold the sides of the sleeve around this inner lining until they meet in the middle, creating a seam. Blind stitch or overhand stitch this seam, press, and then pull out the basting threads.

When all the sleeves have been constructed, attach them to the banner. Put the two ends of the sleeve together to form a loop. Place these ends where marked on the banner, matching the edges of the end seam allowances of the sleeve with that of the banner turning. Sew the sleeve firmly into place.

After all sleeves have been attached, turn under the seam allowances of the lining, baste, press, and fit the lining to the back of the banner. Blind stitch around all the outside edges.

Pocket seam. The banner may also be hung from a rod or bracket that is threaded through a pocket seam. Fit the lining into place, turning under the seam allowances. Baste the front and the lining together, preferably by catching the edges of both pieces of fabric rather than stitching front to back through the layers of material, because sometimes the needle holes will show after the basting threads are removed. Blind stitch the lining into place, leaving an opening on either side where the rod enters and exits. This opening can be at the top of the banner or, if a small heading is desired, about 1 inch from the top edge. Measure down 2 inches from the top edge and sew through all the layers, from one side to the other, in order to create the pocket. If a small heading is desired, sew the first seam 1 inch down from the top edge and the second seam 2 inches below that (or deeper, if the rod is very thick).

Two-sided banners. Banners do not need to be decorated on both sides, but processional banners are much more attractive if they are. A simple design can be done for the back, or a backing of decorative fabric can be used. Constructing a two-sided banner is exactly the same as for the one-sided, with the exception that two inner linings might be needed (one for each side). In this case, be careful to select fabrics that

are not too heavy; the banner must be light enough to carry.

Special considerations for canvaswork. Canvaswork banners will first need to be blocked, but the basic construction techniques remain the same as described above. Lining fabric, however, should be heavier than the lightweight materials used for other banners. Sleeves, if used, should be made from the lining fabric rather than the ground fabric. Display mounting is the same as described.

Displaying Banners

Mounting on a wall (a). Attach to a wall two hooks that are adequate to hold the banner rod. (If desired, use three hooks for a banner with sleeves.) Place hooks at a distance appropriate to hold the rod, then simply drop the rod into these hooks. Avoid the method of tying a cord to both ends of the rod and then looping the center of this cord over a single hook in the wall. The banner may hang crookedly, and this manner of hanging takes up space that should be filled by the banner.

Mounting on a processional staff (b). How a banner is mounted on a staff depends on the staff; several types exist. Determine the type used in your congregation, and examine the banners used with that staff to see how they are made and mounted.

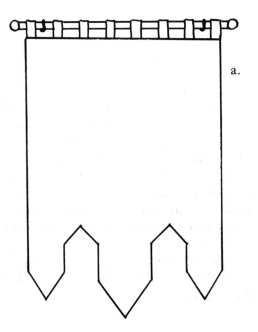

a.

b.

Storing and Maintaining Banners

After banners are finished and have been used, they must be stored and maintained so that they will look fresh and beautiful for years to come.

Storage

When not in use, banners should be hung on long poles in a large cupboard or closet. The hanging poles should be long enough to be threaded through either the sleeves or the pocket of the banner, and they should be specially prepared in order to be acid-free.

Use 1- to 1½-inch pine dowels, which are often used as either curtain rods or clothes closet rods. Sand the poles, seal with three coats of a polyurethane varnish, and then cover with a tube made of preshrunk all-cotton muslin. Hang the embroidered banners on these poles and cover with a muslin dust cloth. The closet should be as airtight as possible and can be lined with cedar to protect against moths. If the closet is not cedar lined, hang bags of cedar shavings from the ceiling, changing them every six to twelve months.

Never store any kind of fabric in plastic bags or sheets of plastic. The plastic does not allow the material to breathe and, because of its high chemical content, may cause damage to the banners.

Maintenance

Banners should be cleaned before storing. Banners should generally not be laundered; vacuuming is the best way to remove ordinary dust. This, however, should be done through a fiberglass screen, holding the screen against the embroidery and running the nozzle of the vacuum across the screen. Screens are easy to construct. Buy fiberglass screening at a hardware store and place it into a double-sided frame of lightweight molding strips. Stretch and staple the screen to the inner surface of one of the sides. Glue the second side of the frame to the first so that the staples and the raw edges of the screening are encased; sand the wood to remove any rough spots; and seal with polyurethane varnish.

A very old method of cleaning goldwork is to rub it with crumbs of white bread, although every iota of crumb must be removed after cleaning so that insects do not attack the embroidery or its ground fabric. It is easier and safer to send the embroidery, even with heavy goldwork, to a reputable dry cleaner. Dry cleaning will seldom be needed, however, if vacuuming is done regularly and the pieces are stored properly.

Keeping the banners dust-free and correctly stored will prolong their lives by many, many years and will greatly reduce the need for repairs.

If any freshening of the banners is needed, use a small hand-held steamer, taking care to hold the steamer vertically so it will not spit water. Silk will waterspot, so exercise the utmost caution. Try steaming the lining side first; that alone may be sufficient. If the banner still is wrinkled, however, steam the front carefully. Never use an iron.

In Conclusion

Banners add beauty and grace to the nave just as do stained-glass windows and flowers. Banners are meant to complement the paraments and vestments and reinforce the meanings of the liturgical seasons. They are an inheritance from ecclesiastical history and a time-tested method of conveying the word of God to the assembled worshipers.

Carefully designed banners skillfully worked of good quality materials offer an excellent opportunity for designers and stitchers to display their talents and to contribute something of themselves to the congregation. Stitching for the house of God is indeed an act of worship. God bless the hearts and hands that beautify the church.